MW01381926

SATURN'S RETURN

Onyia Ali
www.onyiatheoriginal.com

ISBN: 9798846677432
Printed in the United States of America

Cover Design: Onyia Ali
Layout: Onyia Ali
Illustrations: Natali Waters

"no mud, no lotus"

DEDICATED TO MY MOTHER
AND MY DAUGHTER

TABLE OF CONTENTS

introduction

The planet Saturn in astrology is all about tough love and hard work. It represents responsibility, discipline, boundaries, structure, patience, and maturity. During your Saturn return, the moment Saturn returns to the exact placement it was in when you were born, all of these areas of your life are put to the test, and major transformation happens. This period of your life exposes the cracks in your identity and holds up a painfully clear mirror forcing you to re-evaluate and elevate everything in your life.

This collection of poems is a journey through my late twenties while I experienced some of the lowest lows and highest highs of my life. I moved across the country twice, fell in love, had a baby, got my heart broken, lost myself, started two businesses, found my tribe, and took a leap of faith into my full creative power.

These poems are raw, real frozen moments in time that I've kept private... until now. Being vulnerable is never easy, but one of the biggest lessons I've learned during my Saturn return is that being REAL is all that really matters.

I hope my words reassure you that you are not alone in feeling what you feel. I hope they can encourage you to do the work to become the best possible version of yourself and empower you to completely and unapologetically love yourself because when we understand and respect our power, we can do literally anything.

We all know this in our hearts and minds, but sometimes it takes hearing it from someone else to truly get it. So, this is your reminder. No matter where you're at in life, no matter what challenges you're facing, no matter who you have or don't have in your corner... YOU got this.

YOU have the power to choose faith over fear. You have the capacity to focus on gratitude. You have the ability to trust in God, the universe, or whatever higher power you believe in to guide you through this messy, beautiful, complex human experience. It will NOT be easy, but it WILL be worth it. I'm living, breathing proof of that.

Keep going.

xo, Onyia the Original

"You're a Queen baby girl,
go make yourself proud"

THE FOOL

only twenty-five

I'm only 25. Why do I feel like I'm behind?
I'm grown, on my own
You know, tryna stay alive
The momentum of this time
Got me caught up in my mind
I'm not great, I'm not rich
To my future I am blind

I'm only 25. Not even halfway through this life
Checking standards of my peers
Thinkin "Damn, my shit ain't right"
Working every day and night
Just to be "somebody" right?
Fuck this hustle, when's my time
Man I'm tired of this grind

I'm only 25. That's their #1 advice
"You're a baby, you're so young"
But I've died a thousand times
I've cried a thousand times
Tryna get to what is mine
Never easy, always worth it
All my life I had to fight

I'm only 25. In my eyes, you see the drive
To be better, to be worthy
More than life – I wanna thrive
Now I'm focused on MY time
No two lives are just alike
Ain't no blueprint for this shit
But the tops gone be so bright

I'm only 25. Just a nickel and two dimes
But I'm worth my weight in gold
Earning interest in my prime
They be sayin "Girl you fine. You get better just like wine"
So I'm patient and I'm faithful
Cause God's my bottom-line

I'm only 25. But that number's not a guide
Live your life on your own time
And you're guaranteed to shine
Keep your head up and just climb
That's when everything aligns
Gotta pace, fuck a race
Everything will turn out fine

XII

THE HANGEDMAN

you used to be

You used to be my favorite company
Wrapped around your sweet starburst lips
You tasted of love, of life, of passion
When you palmed the soft spots of my hips

You used to be the one to comfort me
Numbing my worries, blinding my pain
You listened to my heart without a word
Do you remember when you kissed me in the rain?

You used to be my inspiration
Melodies shifting my frequency higher
Lost in your voice, your eyes through mine
Yearning for more than temporary desire

You used to be a source of foundation
Supporting like soil beneath my feet
You silently believed in all my dreams
What we had seemed so concrete

You used to be the one I secretly wanted
Afraid to speak about love in your presence
I kept my tongue trapped behind my teeth
As to not accidentally ask for acceptance

You used to be a pharaoh, I saw you King
But in your eyes I was never your Queen
Now you're howling at the moon alone
So I'll love you from a distance, Wolverine

NINE OF WANDS

gods plan

What do you do when you come to a crossroads?
You know, a fork in your life with no way to go

Do you straighten up to stand and fight
Or turn your back and begin your flight?

When the world is testing you
Pressing you
Pulling you thin
Do you figure it out
Or do you just give in?

I like to push my mind from one end to the next
Feeling it burn and breathing through the stretch

I exhale my woes and worries
I expel my wisps of doubt
And sink deeper, fuller, clearer
Affirming that "It will all work out"

But often I'm looking up
Searching for something that's unseen
Asking why and what and where
Questioning what this all means

But then a sign is sent
And again direction's clear
Time to put my faith to test
As my purpose is growing near

So I'm unchaining all control
Over the plans I think I've made
Following the inevitable path
That God has deliberately laid

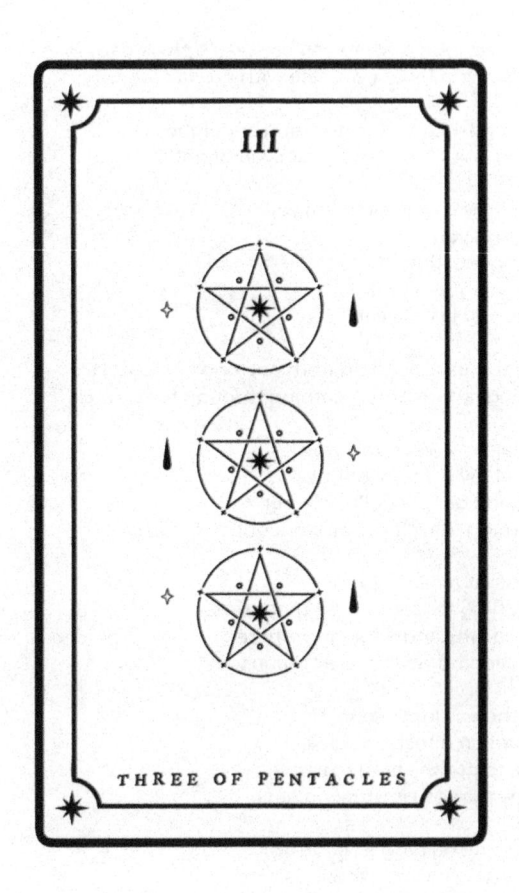

THREE OF PENTACLES

it takes a village

Why is it so hard to ask for help?
Why does the sting of pride swell to my throat
And choke me with resistance
Saying don't rock the boat

I say I need to be strong, as I always have
To prove the relentless soul that I tell myself I am

The thickness of my skull doesn't protect my fragile heart,
though
Preventing the expansion of my mind
Limiting my untethered potential

Why is it so hard not to judge myself?
Like, accepting reality for what it presents to be
Without looking at failure as a measure of me
And seeing my struggle objectively

I know I'm blessed, beyond
And I'm more than just right now
But the grip around my tongue tastes a lot like my ego

Why is it so hard to breathe
To ask for what you need
To cry on a shoulder
Or to admit that you bleed

Why do we succumb to "The Dream"
Comparing ourselves with others needs
With the weight of the world on our shoulders
Trying desperately not to fall to our knees

We pretend to be perfect
Pretend to be pristine
But we gotta remember
We're in this together
It takes a village to succeed

PAGE OF SWORDS

unknown love

Unknown Love, I can almost see your face now
But there's a fog between
Who I am and who I will be

You see, I'm a swaying cocoon clinging to a leaf
But I'm growing for you
And for me

Unknown Love, I'm saturating my wings in color
You'll see how graceful I've become
But for now, I'm rising above
I hope you are too
I want us to
Master solitude

Because how powerful would it be if
We needed ourselves
As much as we needed each other?

Unknown Love, I want my wings to be as strong as my
lungs
So that I'm beyond just beauty alone
See, I'm a Queen, a Monarch
Almost ready for her throne

So I'm praying for YOU
The one by my side
The one down to ride
You know, down to fly

Unknown Love, you only appear in a dream
Hidden by my fear and insecurity
But I love you already
So I pray that you wait for me

I hope that you're patient
And so am I
I know that when eventually I start to flutter
You'll be there to help me fly

awe of you

The waves of the pacific
Have pulled me out to sea
Struggling not to get lost
In this new found we

I've held onto this love
For way too long now
That I'm anxious to give it
Before I even know how

Dazed in this feeling
I'm spinning towards you
You changed my perception
You became my muse

I'm high off your aura
I see its bright blue
I'm sure of your future
You got the best view

So forgive me if I
Don't know what to say
I'm in awe of you
ALL of you
In every single way

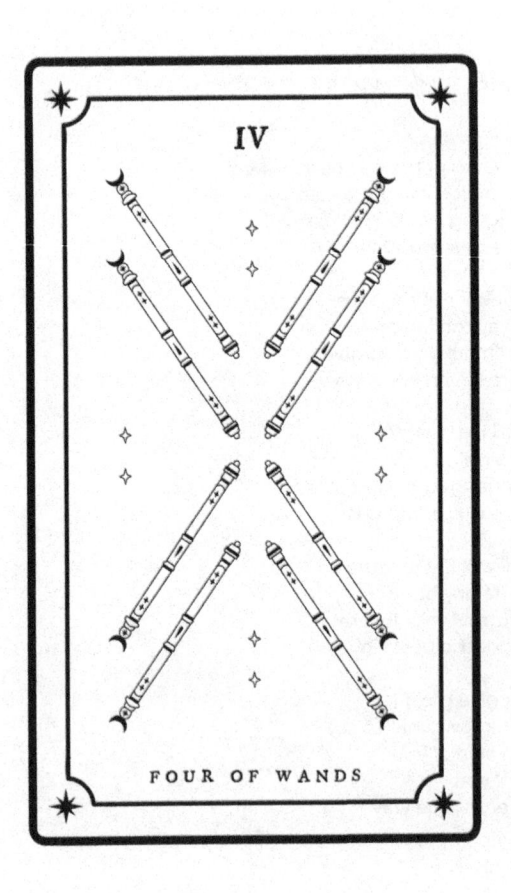

FOUR OF WANDS

amazing grace

You gave me the chance to think bigger than me
Taught me how to see this world unselfishly

I thought I had control
& this life was only mine
Until you came to be
I was searching for a sign

You gave me a chance to know endless love
A blessing of life
Straight from above

I used to be lost
Seeking purpose & meaning
So when God sent me you
I thought I was dreaming

The plan he has can't be ignored
The window of one life closed
Then he opened up this door

I haven't seen your face
Though I know how sweet it is
You're half of each our hearts
Half of mine & half of his

I can't wait to hold you
To kiss your little face
You saved me from myself, Eva
You're my own amazing grace

XI

STRENGTH

you're beautiful, mama

You're beautiful, Mama
 I know it's hard to see
So focused on your baby
Cause now it's "we" not "me"

You're beautiful, Mama

From the inside out
Raising a Queen
Shouldn't be raising a doubt
That you're beautiful, Mama

I know you're kind of lost
Tryna find your way back home
Through the piercing sheer exhaust

But you ARE beautiful, Mama

Your body gave you life
Gave you love you never knew
You are magic
You are light
You are beautiful, Mama

Not the same anymore
You thought you lost your shine
But you're BRIGHTER than before

Yeah, you're beautiful, Mama

From your head to your toes
You're perfectly imperfect
Your aura, it glows

You. are. beautiful. Mama.

And after all that you've been through
Don't forget you're still a woman
Don't forget that you're still YOU

THREE OF SWORDS

wilted red rose

I'm a wilted red rose with thorns
It was a delicate, deadly demise
I slowly lost the will to stand
I started to shrink in size

Without the sun upon my face
Darkness swallowed me whole
It drained me of my energy
It latched onto my soul

They always see my pretty petals
Blind to the danger below
I try to warn them of my flaws
And teach them how I grow

But when they reach to feel my stem
Their wonder turns to pain
And the beauty they once saw in me
Is no longer worth the gain

All I needed was some water
And a few moments in the light
But I cut you too many times
Now I'm out of sight out of mind

IX

THE HERMIT

do you even see me?

Do you even see me?
Am I even here?
I'm slowly fading from your view
About to disappear

I know I'm not the same
And everything has changed

Some days I wish I could go back
And do it all again

But with you, I don't feel safe
There's less love every day
You make me feel like nothing now
Feels like I'm out of place

I'm tired of pretending
Brave facing to the world

When all I really want
Is NOT to be your girl

I need to find myself again
I miss the one I was

The one who was a light
In this dark and crazy world

I'm falling into night
Fading all the way to black

What happened to my joy
Just want the old me back

FIVE OF CUPS

all of you

I wanted ALL of you
That's all it came down to
I wanted every part
Even ones you never knew

I just wanted more
Than you even had to give
Would've swam in your soul
Just to see how you lived

I wanted all of you
The good and the ugly
I wanted who you were
Never cared about the money

What I wanted was too much
For the man you were back then
But I'm praying for your heart
If we ever meet again

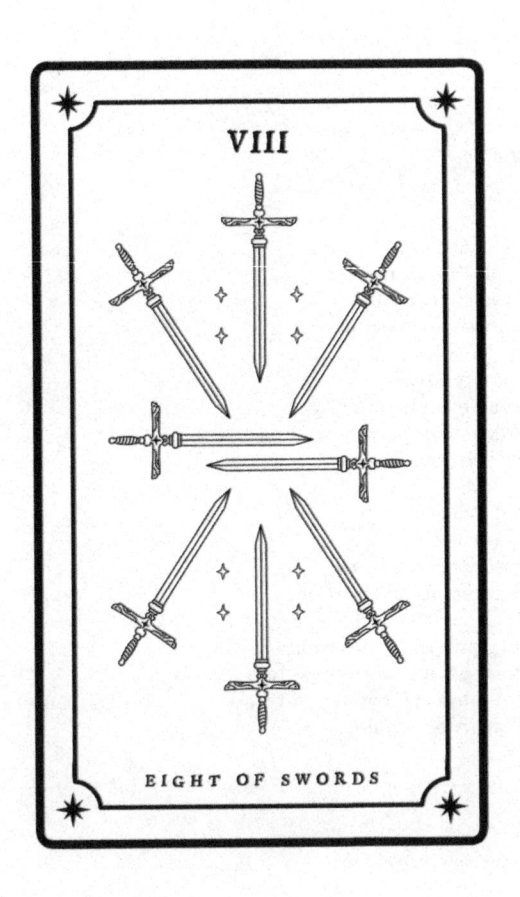

too much woman

Sometimes I feel like
I'm not enough

Not to myself
But to everyone else

My self-love is so strong
I assume I'm the shit
Without a single soul having to tell me I'm "it"

Everyone thinks being pretty makes life fun
But how do you love when "pretty"'s all that they want

They don't want the responsibility
Of what's beneath

They don't want to know what's real

They'd rather make me a fantasy
Then make me a lifelong deal

It's really not that I'm not enough
It's that I'm way too much

Too much strength
Too much wisdom
Too much woman to love

QUEEN OF PENTACLES

regular girl

I'm just a regular girl
By current social rules
I don't have a Birkin
Or a neck full of jewels
My body is all natural
It's been stretched and worn
I didn't get a "mommy makeover"
After my blessing was born

I'm just a regular girl
I don't care who likes me
I'd rather gossip about goals
Than talk about "tea"
I'd rather be showered with love
Than bribed with money
I'd rather work for myself
Than build someone elses legacy

See, I'm just a regular girl
From the outside looking in
With stretch marks and cellulite
And consistently imperfect skin
I'm not an IG model
I don't do shit for clout
And now that I have a baby
Y'all will rarely catch me out

I'm just a regular girl
Trying not to compare online
Cause my body and my life
Are God's unique design
So I'm anything BUT regular
When you look at it that way
I'm perfectly imperfectly myself
And that's more than okay

THE MAGICIAN

rebirth

I've slept on myself for far too long
Shrinking inside to prove that I'm strong
Staying silent to avoid being wrong
Denying my needs just to say I belong

Man, I'm tired of underestimating myself
Underplaying my potential wealth
Undervaluing my precious health
Putting my purpose on a dusty ass shelf

Subscribing to fear had me really fucked up
Had me pouring my soul into someone else's cup
Scared to be proud of my own come ups
Like who I actually was just wasn't enough

I really used to think I wasn't pretty
Not in my eyes, but in the ones I wanted to see me

See, a little validation goes a long way
A compliment can be better than a whole bouquet
A smile could really change someone's day
And self-love really keeps depression away

Now, I know it's not easy waking up to your worth
Trusting in faith and putting yourself first
But if I've learned anything from all this hurt
Is that it's never too late for a muthafuckin rebirth

THE HIGH PRIESTESS

taking back my throne

Inspiration always comes in mysterious ways
But I've struggled to find light in the darkest of days

When my pen hits the paper
The ink disappears
I succumb to my doubts
And I'm swallowed by fear

It's almost as though I forgot who I was
Like I'm not a creative
Like it ain't in my blood

I allowed myself to be set adrift
In an ocean so deep
I didn't even know what I missed

It took me a while to get back here
It took inspiration from a modern Shakespeare

I had to dig deep to recognize my soul
To remember the things that kept me whole

I'll NEVER again dim my light
For anyone afraid of me shining bright

I am a Phoenix
I am the fire
I'm finally someone who I admire

I may not be perfect
But dammit I'm ME
And that also means expression through poetry

So like it or love it
Or leave me alone
I'm taking my seat back on the muthafuckin throne

ACE OF CUPS

love again

I'd be lying if I said I wasn't scared of love
Been slept on, been stepped on
Been taken advantage of

Heart broken so many times
By the ones I loved the most
Now that shit is cold and bare
Love's a memory, a ghost

It haunts me every night
When I lie down all alone
Cause what good is being a Queen
When you're lonely on your throne?

Now I don't even know
Whether it's them or it's me
Who's more toxic than a girl
Who only wants to flee

I'm trying y'all, I am
I wanna believe in love
But I'm bruised, I'm broken
Pray for healing from above

Pray for patience for my heart
And patience for these men
Who be trying to love me now
And I refuse to let them in

One day I'll meet a man
Who will sit with me and wait
Willing to show me that with love
It's never really too late

One day I'll meet a man
Who can love me through this pain
Who can melt this ice cold heart
And teach me how to love again

FOUR OF CUPS

he saw me

He saw my magic
And celebrated it

He wasn't scared of my power
He inhaled it

He had a vision of beauty
And said it was me

He held my heart
Said it was okay to bleed

He tied his soul to mine
When he looked into my eyes

He empowered my mind
And dispelled the lies

He told me I was perfect
He kissed all of my flaws

Then I woke from my dream
And cried for what never was

my toxic trait

My toxic trait is that I like men who don't like me back
You know, the ones who play games and emotionally lack

The trauma from my past distorts my point of view
Making me see potential in something that ain't true

I love to cater, but I need a better plan
I can't be rubbin niggas feet who won't even hold my hand

My toxic trait is that I always see the good
Living in a fantasy
Literally wishing a man would

Overlooking all the ones who do
ALL the things I need them to
Why do I do that?

My toxic trait is that my worth becomes negotiable
In the face of love
My value becomes disposable

I put my needs on hold so that I can help YOU win
But who's helping me feel supported within?

I gotta do better
I owe that to myself
That's why right now my priority is my wealth

Cause y'all be lying
But the numbers don't
& I can love me WAY better than anyone who won't

I owe it to my daughter
To show her what's real
To teach her how to love without getting caught up in the feels

I need her to know that even when we're down
It may slip a little
But we NEVER drop our crown

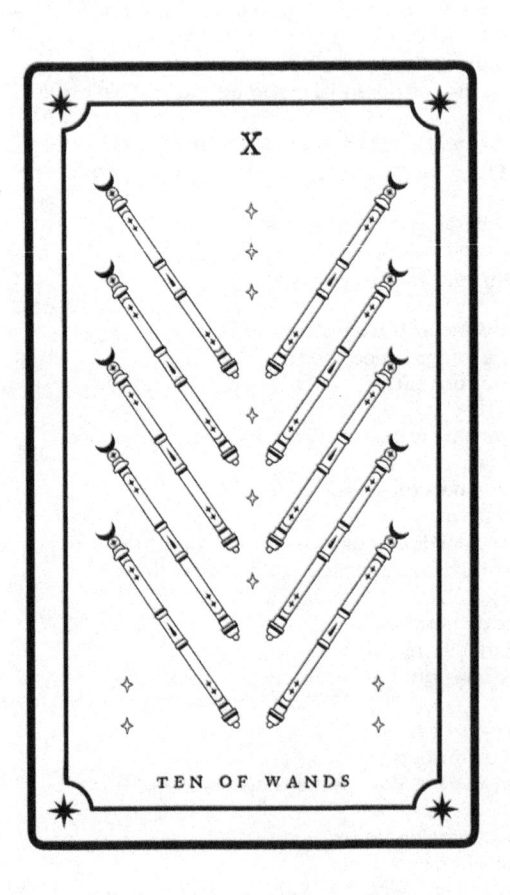

TEN OF WANDS

plant love

Okay let's talk about it sis...
Talk about why we're like this

Let's discuss the ways in which
We shoot our shot & then we miss

Why the nice ones get dismissed
Why we fumble then get pissed

Why WE ain't even got the qualities that we list

Nah let's really talk about
How this world make us doubt
The power that we hold both inside and out

How love can put us on a whole different route
But returning to ourselves is real life clout

How we show up is how we are seen
So mean what you say and say what you mean

Own up to your shit so you can get clean
So you can be a healthy part of the team

We're all a little toxic in our own way
But healing is a choice at the end of the day

Your karma will reflect the seeds you lay
So be sure to plant love in your soil today

submissive

So what do y'all think being submissive is?
Cause I see a lot of definitions that don't seem to fit it

Webster says it's to obey someone else's will
Like let them lead and your needs gotta chill

For some that's triggering, but I don't see nothing wrong
Submission is a two way street
In something that's STRONG

As long as there's plenty of love and respect
You shouldn't have to worry about neglect

I can admit this is something I wanna work on
I've felt the need to be dominant for way too long

But you have to feel safe to truely submit
And I just don't often experience this

To me this isn't even a gender thing
But if I'm a Queen
I'm ONLY submitting to a King

A man about his word who follows through
Who shows no matter what that hes got you

A partner who admits when they are wrong
Who builds you up when you don't feel strong

A leader that's worthy of the title
Who's existence isn't in denial

A man who is a King understands the assignment
That it's not about control, it's about alignment

Cause sometimes you need the Queen to lead
To give you advice, to plant a lil seed

Like I said, submission is a two way street
A place where both people are willing to meet

KING OF SWORDS

take me out the game

I'm just waiting on someone who's real
Someone who ain't afraid to tell me how they feel

I'm waiting on a man who can take the lead
Who can put ego aside to love me how I need

I ain't askin for a lot I just wanna be seen
I want to be visible in this world full of dreams

I've spent enough time shrinking to fit
This perfect mold that was never it

Look, I'm a different type of woman
And I crave a different man
I ain't impressed with ya money
I wanna feel the warmth of your hand

I want ALL your flaws
All your fucked up human ways
As long as it's real
Like honesty all ways

I want everything you are
Without reservation or fear
Transparently yourself
Truth on crystal clear

I want a love so bold that people stare
That the girls start asking me about MY prayer

I need a man Superior in his ways
Never too proud to give me praise

A reflection of myself, my true twin flame?
It's gone take a cold muthafuka to take me out the game

JUDGEMENT

discernment

I know I'm not alone when I say
I need to work on my discernment
I need to learn to judge better
What is and ain't important

Cause what's for me
Will always be
But I gotta have vision
So that I can see clearly

I can't even lie
I've been blinded by lust
Been caught up with niggas
That I damn sure shouldn't trust

Cause it shouldn't be enough
To just like my face
My presence is a gift
I don't have vibes to waste

So I'm paying closer attention
With my heart set on intention
Taking time to ground myself
Call it a self love intervention

I'm not sorry I'm selective
I'm protective of my energy
I deserve absolutely nothing less
Than respect and reciprocity

I have a right to set my boundaries
And I'm worth the time it takes
To learn to trust myself
To give myself a little grace

With God in my corner
And intuition on my side
I can use the power of discernment
To feel solid, fortified

And what could be more powerful
Than knowing what you need?
Knowing that you always have it in you
To find peace, guaranteed

never again

Never again will I
Put profit over peace
Love is not enough
The price has been increased

Never again will I
Accept what's not for me
I know that I'm a Queen
A divine priority

Never again will I
Question my own worth
Or the value that I bring
I know what I deserve

Never again will I
Try to dim my light
For anyone or anything
That cannot see me shine

THE HIEROPHANT

dope in real life

Social media really got the game fucked up
We fighting for attention but they got ours stuck

Comparing our flaws to a Photoshop
Being sold that we'll never be perfect enough

It's crazy cause we know perfect doesn't exist
But we all still subscribe to this fuckin matrix

Scrolling our screens like zombies
Being influenced to feel like we're incomplete
So we can buy whatever they say we need
Cause our reality ain't as cool as the next feed

What if we put our phones down
And opened our eyes
To the beauty of life being lived outside

Our existence doesn't always have to be seen
And you can't sum it up for a tiny phone screen

Our lives are SO valuable
Even the mundane
Not in how many likes or followers we obtain

This game is to be played
But we're the ones who are
We forget that in reality
WE are the star

So don't let this shit stop you from shining bright
Baby, the real flex is being dope in REAL life

XV

THE DEVIL

shadow work

How can you see the light
When you've never been in darkness
How can you find yourself
When you're lost without a compass

The measure of your healing
Is NOT the peace you find
It's the discovery of truth
That resides within your mind

How well do you know your shadow?
You know, the ugliness inside
The scary broken pieces
That you desperately try to hide

We ALL are complex beings
Full of darkness and of light
So we need to be AWARE
More than we need to be right

Dive deep into your soul
To understand the purest you
To unlearn all the false beliefs
That you truly thought you knew

Cause when we find acceptance
For the wholeness of our souls
We get to rebuild our reality
From the damaging inner lies told

Being human can get messy
So be brave and uncover your worth
Self-love is SO important
But so is shadow work

WHEEL OF FORTUNE

karma good af

I know my karma is good as fuck
And when I say karma I mean energy, vibe, and luck

But that ain't something I was just born with
I had to plant seeds of good to see that benefit

What goes around comes around
We all know that
The universe pays attention
That's a cold hard fact

You gotta be intentional about the way you show up
So that all that's meant for you
Can overflow your cup

They say karma is a bitch and I agree
You get what you give, that's a guarantee

You ever done somebody wrong and it comes back to bite you?
You ever doubted yourself and the plans you made fall through?

The energy we maintain
Determines the blessings that we gain
It's our faith that must remain
Despite the struggle and the pain

The goal of life is not perfection
It's making mistakes
And then making corrections

It's checking our energy when shit gets weird
And adjusting our vibration to a higher tier

We all have the power to elevate and grow
But be mindful with your choices
Cause you reap what you sow

pain into profit

Turning pain into profit is my favorite profession
Went from a broken hearted girl
To instant progression

I took the darkness felt inside
Put it towards my accession
Now the worlds looking at me from a different perspective

I'm a diamond in the rough
But I was afraid to shine
Afraid that no one would ever truely see my light

I was convinced that I just wasn't enough
Unskilled, unspoken, unpolished, and rough

Like who really cares what I have to say
I'm just a nobody at the end of the day

But what y'all have shown me goes far beyond words
It's not just how I use nouns and verbs

My talent for truth gives a voice to the voiceless
It empowers & inspires our collective success

I see y'all standing up
And standing strong
And it reminds me it wasn't just me all along

So thank you for coming on this journey with me
I think I'm finally
Exactly
Where I'm supposed to be

QUEEN OF CUPS

queen

Hell yeah I'm a Queen
So you know what that means
I water my own grass
So it always stays green

And I keep my crown on
Even if it's unseen

See, royalty is in my blood
I'm blessed but I still get it out the mud

I got God's plan
That's real love
So failure ain't even something I'm thinking of

The purpose in me is far too great
To sit and hope and wish and wait
A Queen expands what she creates
Walking fearlessly towards her divine fate

I'm a Monarch
And I know how to fly
When y'all go low, I'm already on high
When y'all try me, there's no need for a reply
I see and feel everything through my third eye

On days when I feel like I don't fit the genre
I hype myself up when I really don't wanna
Reminding my soul "You're beautiful Mama"
"You got a nice ass & some good fuckin karma"

Some days we'll have to adjust our crown
It starts to slip when we feel like we're down

Plant your feet in the earth and find solid ground
You're a Queen, babygirl
Go make yourself proud

big oshun energy

I got big Oshun energy
And no I won't apologize
I'm at a peaceful place in life where
I am both beautiful and wise

A goddess that brings life and light
To every place she goes
Oshun harnesses her feminine power
Her strength AND sensuality flows

Like the water she sweetens
Creating abundant seasons
And harvesting her own fruit for the eating

She is power FULL
Full of magic
Full of promise
Full of life
And we all have a little of this energy
We just have to tap into it right?

As women we have work to do
To rediscover all that's been lost
Through years of patriarchal bullshit
We're now challenging what we thought

I am a woman
A goddess
A Queen
And I refuse to just play a part
There is value in my heart and mind
There is value in my art

But as special as I know I am
I'm also humble enough to know
That without my community
I never would have been able to grow

So reach out and find your sisterhood
Because we all have so much to give
And together we can create a world
That's a more empowering place to live

XXI

THE WORLD

saturn return

My late twenties exposed
I'm kinda rough on the edges
They showed my entirety
My depth of expression

I learned to see failures
As micro-progressions
And that trusting the process
Yields the sweetest successes

For so long I felt so broken inside
I felt I had to hide
Had to dim my light
Cause if you wanna fit in
You can't shine TOO bright
Especially if you're pretty
You gotta humble yourself, right?

At the beginning, I almost ended it all
20 years old and lost without a cause
I felt worthless
Unloveable
Not fit for this life
So I grabbed a razor and some pills that night

And by the grace of God, I'm still here
A decade later going into my 30th year

But what I know now
That I didn't back then
Is that there is ALWAYS light at the tunnel's end

There is purpose in all this chaos and pain
There's connection deeper that we can explain

All these years I thought
That life was breaking me
The universe was preparing
And molding
And making me

Each and every piece from my broken heart
Now creates this beautiful mosaic art

So although I've had some tough lessons to learn
I am so fucking grateful for my Saturn return

Made in the USA
Columbia, SC
07 November 2023

25249244R00043